HOLIDAY TREATS

Delicious Recipes for all holiday

by Andrii Pysarenko

Disclaimer

The information provided in this cookbook is intended for educational and informational purposes only. The author is not a professional chef or nutritionist. While every effort has been made to ensure the accuracy of the information contained within this book, the author assumes no responsibility or liability for any errors or omissions, nor for the use or misuse of the information provided.

The recipes and cooking techniques in this book are meant to be used as guidelines. The author does not guarantee any specific outcome as cooking conditions, ingredients, and equipment may vary. Please use your direction and take into account any dietary restrictions or food allergies.

The author and publisher disclaim any liability for any adverse effects or consequences arising directly or indirectly from use of the information or recipes contained in this book. Always follow safety guidelines and appliance instructions, and seek professional advice when needed.

CONTENTS

Appetizers

APPETIZERS

1. <u>Stuffed Mushrooms</u> — Mushrooms stuffed with breadcrumbs, cheese, and garlic, then baked to perfection.
2. <u>Deviled Eggs</u> — Hard-boiled eggs mixed with mayo, mustard, and spices.
3. <u>Bacon-Wrapped Asparagus</u> — Fresh asparagus wrapped in crispy bacon and roasted.
4. <u>Cheese Platter</u> — Assorted cheeses with crackers, nuts, and fresh fruits.
5. <u>Spinach Artichoke Dip</u> — A creamy dip served with tortilla chips or toasted baguette slices.
6. <u>Shrimp Cocktail</u> — Poached shrimp served with a tangy cocktail sauce.
7. <u>Stuffed Mini Peppers</u> — Mini bell peppers stuffed with cream cheese and herbs.
8. <u>Guacamole and Chips</u> — Fresh avocados, tomatoes, onions, and lime juice served with tortilla chips.
9. <u>Bruschetta</u> — Toasted baguette topped with fresh tomatoes, basil, and balsamic glaze.
10. <u>Cranberry Brie Bites</u> — Puff pastry filled with brie cheese and cranberry sauce.

INGREDIENTS

- 20 large mushrooms, stems removed
- 1 cup breadcrumbs
- ½ cup grated Parmesan cheese
- 2 cloves garlic, minced
- 2 tablespoons parsley, chopped
- ¼ cup cream cheese
- 2 tablespoons butter, melted
- Salt and pepper to taste
- 1 tablespoon olive oil
- ¼ cup shredded mozzarella cheese

PREPARATION

- **Preheat the Oven:** Preheat your oven to 375°F (190°C).
- **Prepare the Mushrooms:** Clean the mushrooms and remove the stems, setting them aside.
- **Make the Filling:** In a bowl, mix the breadcrumbs, Parmesan cheese, minced garlic, cream cheese, parsley, salt, and pepper. Add the melted butter and stir until combined.
- **Fill the Mushrooms:** Spoon the filling into each mushroom cap, packing it in gently.
- **Top with Cheese:** Sprinkle shredded mozzarella cheese on top of the filled mushrooms.
- **Bake:** Place the mushrooms on a baking sheet, drizzle lightly with olive oil, and bake for 15-20 minutes, or until the tops are golden brown.
- **Serve:** Garnish with extra parsley if desired and serve warm.

Deviled Eggs

INGREDIENTS

- **6 large eggs, hard-boiled and peeled**
- **3 tablespoons mayonnaise**
- **1 teaspoon Dijon mustard**
- **1 teaspoon vinegar (white or apple cider vinegar)**
- **Salt and pepper to taste**
- **Paprika for garnish**
- **1 teaspoon pickle relish (optional)**
- **1 teaspoon hot sauce (optional)**
- **1 tablespoon chives, finely chopped (for garnish)**

PREPARATION

- **Boil the Eggs:** Hard-boil the eggs by placing them in a saucepan, covering them with water, and bringing them to a boil. Once boiling, turn off the heat, cover, and let sit for 10-12 minutes. Drain and cool under cold water.
- **Slice the Eggs:** Peel the eggs and slice them in half lengthwise. Gently remove the yolks and place them in a small bowl.
- **Prepare the Filling:** Mash the yolks with a fork and mix in the mayonnaise, mustard, vinegar, salt, and pepper. If desired, add pickle relish or hot sauce for extra flavor.
- **Fill the Egg Whites:** Spoon or pipe the yolk mixture back into the egg white halves.
- **Garnish:** Sprinkle the tops with paprika and garnish with chives.
- **Chill and Serve:** Refrigerate for at least 15 minutes before serving.

Bacon-Wrapped Asparagus

INGREDIENTS

- 20 asparagus spears, trimmed
- 10 slices bacon, cut in half
- 1 tablespoon olive oil
- Salt and pepper to taste
- 1 teaspoon garlic powder
- ½ teaspoon onion powder
- 1 teaspoon balsamic vinegar (optional)
- 1 teaspoon honey (optional)
- Fresh parsley for garnish
- ¼ teaspoon red pepper flakes (optional)

PREPARATION

- **Preheat the Oven:** Preheat your oven to 400°F (200°C).
- **Prepare the Asparagus:** Wash and trim the ends of the asparagus spears.
- **Wrap with Bacon:** Take half a slice of bacon and wrap it around each asparagus spear, starting at one end and spiraling to the other. Secure with toothpicks if necessary.
- **Season:** Arrange the bacon-wrapped asparagus on a baking sheet. Drizzle with olive oil and season with salt, pepper, garlic powder, and onion powder. Add red pepper flakes for a bit of heat, if desired.
- **Bake:** Bake for 12-15 minutes until the bacon is crispy and the asparagus is tender.
- **Optional Glaze:** Mix honey and balsamic vinegar together and brush it over the bacon-wrapped asparagus in the last 5 minutes of cooking for added flavor.
- **Garnish and Serve:** Remove from the oven, garnish with fresh parsley, and serve warm.

Cheese Platter

INGREDIENTS

- Cheeses:
- 6-8 ounces Brie cheese
- 6-8 ounces sharp Cheddar cheese
- 6-8 ounces Gouda cheese
- (Optional: blue cheese, goat cheese, or a soft cheese like Camembert)
- Crackers:
- Assorted crackers (water crackers, whole wheat crackers, or artisan crackers)
- Fruits:
- Fresh grapes (red or green)
- **Fresh berries (strawberries, blackberries, or blueberries)**
- Sliced apples or pears
- **Dried fruits (apricots, figs, or dates)**
- Nuts:
- Mixed nuts (almonds, walnuts, pecans)
- Candied nuts (optional)
- Extras:
- 2-3 types of charcuterie (e.g., prosciutto, salami, or chorizo)
- Honey or jam (for drizzling or dipping)
- Fresh herbs (rosemary, thyme, or mint) for garnish
- Olives (optional)

PREPARATION

- **Choose a Platter or Board:** Use a large wooden board, marble slab, or a serving tray as your base for the cheese platter.
- **Arrange the Cheeses:** Place the different cheeses on the board, spaced out, and leave the soft cheeses whole. Slice harder cheeses like Cheddar and Gouda into thin wedges or cubes.
- **Add Crackers and Bread:** Place a variety of crackers around the cheeses, arranging them in small piles or spreading them out around the board.
- **Place Fresh Fruits and Dried Fruits:** Arrange bunches of grapes, berries, and slices of apples or pears around the cheeses. Add dried fruits like apricots and figs for texture and sweetness.
- **Add Nuts and Extras:** Scatter mixed nuts and candied nuts around the board. Add charcuterie meats in rolled or fanned-out portions for an elegant touch.
- **Include Honey, Jam, and Garnishes:** Place small bowls of honey or jam on the board, along with olives or fresh herbs for garnish. Drizzle honey over soft cheeses like Brie if desired.
- **Final Touches:** Garnish with fresh herbs like rosemary sprigs, and serve with cheese knives for easy cutting.

Spinach Artichoke Dip

INGREDIENTS

- 1 cup fresh spinach, chopped
- 1 cup artichoke hearts, chopped
- ½ cup mayonnaise
- ½ cup sour cream
- 1 cup shredded mozzarella cheese
- ½ cup grated Parmesan cheese
- 2 cloves garlic, minced
- Salt and pepper to taste
- 1 tablespoon olive oil
- Tortilla chips or baguette slices for serving

PREPARATION

- **Preheat the Oven:** Preheat your oven to 350°F (175°C).
- **Sauté the Spinach:** Heat the olive oil in a skillet over medium heat. Add the chopped spinach and cook until wilted (if using fresh). If using frozen spinach, skip this step and make sure it's fully drained.
- **Combine Ingredients:** In a mixing bowl, combine the spinach, chopped artichoke hearts, mayonnaise, sour cream, mozzarella, Parmesan, garlic, salt, and pepper. Stir until well mixed.
- **Transfer to Baking Dish:** Pour the mixture into an oven-safe dish or skillet.
- **Bake:** Bake for 20-25 minutes until the top is golden and bubbly.
- **Serve:** Serve hot with tortilla chips or toasted baguette slices for dipping.

Shrimp Cocktail

INGREDIENTS

- pound large shrimp, peeled and deveined
- Salt to taste
- 1 lemon, sliced
- 1 bay leaf
- 1 cup cocktail sauce
- 1 tablespoon horseradish
- 1 teaspoon Worcestershire sauce
- Fresh parsley for garnish
- 1 cup ice cubes
- 1 teaspoon Old Bay seasoning (optional)

PREPARATION

- **Boil the Shrimp:** Fill a large pot with water and add lemon slices, bay leaf, salt, and peppercorns. Bring to a boil.
- **Poach the Shrimp:** Add the shrimp to the boiling water and cook for 2-3 minutes, until the shrimp turn pink and are cooked through.
- **Chill the Shrimp:** Remove the shrimp and immediately transfer them to an ice bath to stop the cooking process. Let the shrimp chill for 5 minutes.
- **Prepare Cocktail Sauce:** In a bowl, mix the cocktail sauce, horseradish, and Worcestershire sauce until well combined.
- **Serve:** Arrange the chilled shrimp on a serving platter with lemon wedges and a bowl of cocktail

Stuffed Mini Peppers

INGREDIENTS

- 12 mini bell peppers, halved and seeded
- 1 cup cream cheese
- ¼ cup shredded mozzarella cheese
- 2 tablespoons Parmesan cheese, grated
- 2 tablespoons fresh parsley, chopped
- 1 tablespoon chives, chopped
- Salt and pepper to taste
- 1 teaspoon garlic powder
- 1 teaspoon Italian seasoning
- Olive oil spray

PREPARATION

- **Preheat the Oven:** Preheat your oven to 375°F (190°C).
- **Prepare the Peppers:** Cut the mini bell peppers in half lengthwise and remove the seeds.
- **Make the Filling:** In a mixing bowl, combine the cream cheese, mozzarella, Parmesan, parsley, chives, garlic powder, Italian seasoning, salt, and pepper. Mix until smooth.
- **Stuff the Peppers:** Spoon the cream cheese mixture into each mini pepper half, filling them generously.
- **Bake:** Arrange the stuffed peppers on a baking sheet and lightly spray them with olive oil.
- **Bake for 15 Minutes:** Bake for 15-20 minutes, or until the peppers are tender and the cheese is slightly golden on top.
- **Serve:** Remove from the oven and let cool slightly before serving.

Guacamole and Chips

INGREDIENTS

- 3 ripe avocados
- 1 small tomato, diced
- ¼ cup red onion, diced
- 1 tablespoon fresh lime juice
- 1 tablespoon fresh cilantro, chopped
- Salt and pepper to taste
- 1 teaspoon garlic powder
- 1 teaspoon cumin
- 1 small jalapeño, diced (optional)
- Tortilla chips for serving

PREPARATION

- **Prepare the Avocados:** Cut the avocados in half, remove the pits, and scoop the flesh into a mixing bowl.
- **Mash the Avocados:** Mash the avocados with a fork until you reach your desired consistency (chunky or smooth).
- **Add the Vegetables:** Stir in the diced tomato, red onion, jalapeño (if using), cilantro, and lime juice.
- **Season:** Add garlic powder, salt, pepper, and cumin (if using). Taste and adjust seasoning as needed.
- **Serve:** Transfer the guacamole to a serving bowl and serve with tortilla chips.

INGREDIENTS

- 1 baguette, sliced
- 1 cup diced tomatoes
- ¼ cup fresh basil, chopped
- 2 cloves garlic, minced
- 1 tablespoon olive oil
- Salt and pepper to taste
- 1 tablespoon balsamic glaze
- 1 tablespoon Parmesan cheese, grated
- 1 tablespoon fresh parsley, chopped
- Olive oil for brushing

PREPARATION

- **Preheat the Oven:** Preheat your oven to 375°F (190°C).
- **Toast the Baguette:** Brush the baguette slices with olive oil and place them on a baking sheet. Toast in the oven for 5-7 minutes, until golden and crispy.
- **Prepare the Tomato Topping:** In a bowl, combine the diced tomatoes, chopped basil, minced garlic, olive oil, salt, and pepper. Mix well.
- **Assemble the Bruschetta:** Spoon the tomato mixture onto each toasted baguette slice.
- **Drizzle with Balsamic Glaze:** Drizzle balsamic glaze over the bruschetta for a tangy finish.
- **Optional Garnish:** Sprinkle with grated Parmesan cheese and chopped parsley for added flavor and presentation.
- **Serve:** Serve immediately as a fresh, flavorful appetizer.
-

Cranberry Brie Bites

INGREDIENTS

- 1 sheet puff pastry, thawed
- 8 ounces Brie cheese, cut into small cubes
- ½ cup cranberry sauce (homemade or store-bought)
- 1 egg, beaten (for egg wash)
- 1 tablespoon honey (optional)
- ¼ cup chopped walnuts or pecans (optional)
- 1 teaspoon fresh rosemary, chopped (for garnish)
- 1 tablespoon brown sugar (optional)
- 1 teaspoon orange zest (optional)
- Flour for dusting (to prevent sticking)

PREPARATION

- **Preheat the Oven:** Preheat your oven to 375°F (190°C). Lightly grease a mini muffin tin.
- **Prepare the Puff Pastry:** Roll out the puff pastry on a lightly floured surface and cut it into 12 equal squares.
- **Assemble the Bites:** Place each puff pastry square into the wells of the mini muffin tin. Add a small cube of Brie cheese into each pastry square and top with a spoonful of cranberry sauce.
- **Optional Toppings:** Drizzle with honey, sprinkle chopped nuts, or add brown sugar and orange zest if desired.
- **Brush with Egg Wash:** Lightly brush the edges of the puff pastry with the beaten egg to help them turn golden while baking.
- **Bake:** Bake for 12-15 minutes, or until the puff pastry is golden brown and the cheese is melted.
- **Garnish and Serve:** Remove from the oven and garnish with fresh rosemary. Serve warm.

Main Dishes

MAIN DISHES

1. **Roast Turkey** — A classic roast turkey with a simple herb butter rub.
2. **Honey-Glazed Ham** — Baked ham with a sweet honey glaze.
3. **Herb-Crusted Prime Rib** — Prime rib seasoned with herbs and roasted until tender.
4. **Stuffed Turkey Breast** — Turkey breast stuffed with cranberries, herbs, and breadcrumbs.
5. **Garlic Butter Roast Chicken** — Whole chicken roasted with garlic and butter.
6. **Beef Tenderloin** — Simple roasted beef tenderloin seasoned with salt and pepper.
7. **Salmon with Lemon and Dill** — Baked salmon with lemon slices and fresh dill.
8. **Vegetarian Stuffed Acorn Squash** — Roasted acorn squash filled with wild rice, cranberries, and nuts.
9. **Lamb Chops with Rosemary** — Lamb chops seasoned with rosemary and garlic, then pan-seared.
10. **Vegetable Pot Pie** — A flaky pie crust filled with mixed vegetables in a creamy sauce.

Roast Turkey

INGREDIENTS

- 1 whole turkey (12-14 lbs), thawed if frozen
- ½ cup unsalted butter, softened
- 2 tablespoons fresh rosemary, chopped
- 2 tablespoons fresh thyme, chopped
- 4 garlic cloves, minced
- 1 lemon, halved
- 1 onion, quartered
- 2 cups chicken or turkey broth
- Salt and pepper to taste
- Fresh herbs (rosemary, thyme) for garnish (optional

PREPARATION

- **Preheat the Oven:** Preheat your oven to 325°F (165°C).
- **Prepare the Turkey:** Remove the neck and giblets from the turkey cavity, and pat the turkey dry with paper towels.
- **Make the Herb Butter:** In a small bowl, combine the softened butter, chopped rosemary, thyme, garlic, salt, and pepper. Mix until well combined.
- **Rub the Turkey:** Gently loosen the skin of the turkey breast by sliding your hands underneath. Rub half of the herb butter under the skin of the turkey breast and the other half over the entire outside of the turkey.
- **Stuff the Turkey (Optional):** Stuff the cavity of the turkey with the lemon halves, quartered onion, and additional herbs if desired.
- **Truss the Turkey:** Tie the legs together with kitchen twine and tuck the wing tips under the body of the turkey to prevent them from burning.
- **Roast the Turkey:** Place the turkey on a roasting rack in a large roasting pan. Pour the chicken or turkey broth into the bottom of the pan. Cover the turkey loosely with aluminum foil.
- **Roast the Turkey:** Roast the turkey in the preheated oven for about 2 ½ to 3 hours, or until the internal temperature of the turkey reaches 165°F (74°C) in the thickest part of the thigh. Remove the foil in the last 45 minutes to allow the skin to brown and become crispy.
- **Rest the Turkey:** Once the turkey is done, remove it from the oven and let it rest for 20-30 minutes before carving. This allows the juices to redistribute and makes for a juicier turkey.
- **Garnish and Serve:** Garnish with fresh herbs if desired and carve the turkey for serving.

Honey-Glazed Ham

INGREDIENTS

- 1 bone-in ham (8-10 lbs)
- 1 cup honey
- ½ cup brown sugar
- ¼ cup Dijon mustard
- 2 tablespoons apple cider vinegar
- 1 teaspoon ground cloves
- 1 teaspoon ground cinnamon
- ¼ cup orange juice
- Whole cloves for garnish (optional)
- Fresh rosemary for garnish (optional)

PREPARATION

- **Preheat the Oven:** Preheat your oven to 325°F (165°C).
- **Prepare the Ham:** If the ham is not pre-sliced, score the surface of the ham in a diamond pattern by making shallow cuts with a sharp knife. If desired, insert whole cloves into the cross-sections of the cuts.
- **Make the Honey Glaze:** In a small saucepan, combine honey, brown sugar, Dijon mustard, apple cider vinegar, ground cloves, cinnamon, and orange juice. Stir over medium heat until the sugar dissolves and the glaze is smooth. Remove from heat.
- **Glaze the Ham:** Place the ham in a large roasting pan, cut-side down. Brush the ham with about half of the glaze, ensuring it is evenly coated.
- **Bake the Ham:** Cover the ham loosely with aluminum foil and bake in the preheated oven for about 1 ½ to 2 hours, basting every 30 minutes with the remaining glaze.
- **Finish the Glaze:** For a deeper caramelized crust, remove the foil in the last 30 minutes of baking and brush the ham with the last layer of glaze.
- **Check the Temperature:** The ham should be heated through and reach an internal temperature of 140°F (60°C).
- **Rest and Garnish:** Once baked, remove the ham from the oven and let it rest for 15-20 minutes before carving. Garnish with fresh rosemary for a beautiful presentation.

Herb-Crusted Prime Rib

INGREDIENTS

- 1 prime rib roast (5-6 lbs, bone-in or boneless)
- 3 tablespoons olive oil
- 2 tablespoons fresh rosemary, chopped
- 2 tablespoons fresh thyme, chopped
- 5 garlic cloves, minced
- 1 tablespoon Dijon mustard
- 1 teaspoon kosher salt
- 1 teaspoon black pepper
- 1 tablespoon horseradish (optional)
- Fresh herbs for garnish (optional)

PREPARATION

- **Preheat the Oven:** Preheat your oven to 450°F (230°C).
- **Prepare the Prime Rib:** Let the prime rib roast sit at room temperature for 30-60 minutes to ensure even cooking.
- **Make the Herb Rub:** In a small bowl, combine olive oil, rosemary, thyme, garlic, Dijon mustard, salt, pepper, and horseradish (if using). Mix to form a paste.
- **Rub the Prime Rib:** Rub the herb mixture evenly over the entire surface of the prime rib, ensuring that it's fully coated.
- **Roast the Prime Rib:** Place the prime rib on a roasting rack in a large roasting pan, fat-side up. Roast in the preheated oven at 450°F (230°C) for 15 minutes to sear the outside.
- **Lower the Temperature:** Reduce the oven temperature to 325°F (165°C) and continue roasting the prime rib for about 1 ½ to 2 hours, or until the internal temperature reaches 120-125°F (49-52°C) for medium-rare, or 130°F (54°C) for medium. (The temperature will continue to rise as it rests.)
- **Rest the Roast:** Remove the prime rib from the oven and loosely cover it with aluminum foil. Let it rest for 20-30 minutes before carving. Resting allows the juices to redistribute, making the meat tender and juicy.
- **Carve and Serve:** Carve the prime rib into thick slices and garnish with fresh herbs, if desired.

INGREDIENTS

- 1 boneless turkey breast (3-4 lbs)
- ½ cup breadcrumbs
- ¼ cup dried cranberries
- 2 tablespoons fresh parsley, chopped
- 1 tablespoon fresh thyme, chopped
- 2 garlic cloves, minced
- 2 tablespoons butter, melted
- 1 tablespoon olive oil
- Salt and pepper to taste
- Fresh herbs for garnish (optional)

PREPARATION

- **Preheat the Oven:** Preheat your oven to 350°F (175°C).
- **Prepare the Stuffing:** In a mixing bowl, combine the breadcrumbs, dried cranberries, chopped parsley, thyme, minced garlic, melted butter, salt, and pepper. Mix until well combined.
- **Butterfly the Turkey Breast:** Using a sharp knife, butterfly the turkey breast by cutting horizontally through the middle of the breast without cutting all the way through. Open it like a book to create an even layer.
- **Stuff the Turkey Breast:** Spread the prepared stuffing mixture evenly over the inside of the turkey breast.
- **Roll and Secure:** Roll up the turkey breast tightly, starting from one long side. Use kitchen twine to tie the rolled turkey at 2-inch intervals to keep the stuffing inside and the shape intact.
- **Season the Outside:** Rub the outside of the turkey breast with olive oil, salt, and pepper.
- **Roast the Turkey Breast:** Place the rolled turkey breast in a roasting pan, seam side down. Roast for 60-75 minutes, or until the internal temperature of the turkey reaches 165°F (74°C).
- **Rest the Turkey:** Remove the turkey from the oven and let it rest for 10-15 minutes before slicing. Resting allows the juices to redistribute and ensures moist, tender meat.
- **Carve and Serve:** Slice the stuffed turkey breast into rounds and garnish with fresh herbs for a beautiful presentation.

5

Garlic Butter Roast Chicken

INGREDIENTS

- 1 whole chicken (4-5 lbs)
- ½ cup unsalted butter, softened
- 4 garlic cloves, minced
- 1 tablespoon fresh rosemary, chopped
- 1 tablespoon fresh thyme, chopped
- 1 lemon, quartered
- 1 onion, quartered
- Salt and pepper to taste
- 1 tablespoon olive oil
- Fresh parsley for garnish (optional)

PREPARATION

- **Preheat the Oven:** Preheat your oven to 425°F (220°C).
- **Prepare the Garlic Butter:** In a small bowl, mix the softened butter, minced garlic, chopped rosemary, chopped thyme, salt, and pepper.
- **Prepare the Chicken:** Remove the giblets from the chicken cavity, if present, and pat the chicken dry with paper towels.
- **Rub the Chicken with Garlic Butter:** Gently loosen the skin of the chicken breast by sliding your fingers underneath. Rub half of the garlic butter under the skin of the chicken breast and the remaining butter all over the outside of the chicken.
- **Stuff the Chicken (Optional):** Stuff the chicken cavity with the quartered lemon and onion for extra flavor.
- **Truss the Chicken:** Tie the legs together with kitchen twine and tuck the wing tips under the body of the chicken to prevent burning.
- **Roast the Chicken:** Place the chicken breast-side up on a roasting rack in a roasting pan. Drizzle with olive oil and roast in the preheated oven for 1 ½ hours, or until the internal temperature reaches 165°F (74°C) in the thickest part of the thigh. Baste the chicken occasionally with the pan drippings for added flavor.
- **Rest the Chicken:** Once the chicken is done roasting, remove it from the oven and let it rest for 10-15 minutes before carving. Resting allows the juices to redistribute, making the meat tender and juicy.
- **Garnish and Serve:** Carve the chicken and garnish with fresh parsley, if desired. Serve with your favorite side dishes.

6

Beef Tenderloin

INGREDIENTS

- 1 beef tenderloin (2-3 lbs), trimmed of excess fat and silver skin
- 2 tablespoons olive oil
- 1 tablespoon kosher salt
- 1 tablespoon freshly ground black pepper
- 2 garlic cloves, minced (optional)
- 1 tablespoon fresh rosemary, chopped (optional)
- 1 tablespoon unsalted butter
- Fresh herbs for garnish (optional

PREPARATION

- **Preheat the Oven:** Preheat your oven to 425°F (220°C).
- **Season the Tenderloin:** Pat the beef tenderloin dry with paper towels. Rub the entire surface of the tenderloin with olive oil, then season generously with kosher salt and black pepper. If desired, rub minced garlic and chopped rosemary over the beef for extra flavor.
- **Sear the Beef:** Heat a large skillet over medium-high heat. Add 1 tablespoon of olive oil and 1 tablespoon of butter. Once hot, sear the beef tenderloin on all sides for about 2-3 minutes per side, until a golden-brown crust forms.
- **Roast the Beef:** Transfer the seared beef tenderloin to a roasting pan or baking sheet. Roast in the preheated oven for 20-25 minutes for medium-rare (internal temperature of 125-130°F or 52-54°C), or longer if you prefer your meat more well-done. Use a meat thermometer to check the internal temperature.
- **Rest the Tenderloin:** Remove the beef tenderloin from the oven and let it rest on a cutting board for 10-15 minutes. The internal temperature will rise as it rests, and resting helps the juices redistribute, resulting in a tender, juicy roast.
- **Slice and Serve:** Slice the beef tenderloin into thick slices and garnish with fresh herbs if desired

7

Salmon with Lemon and Dill

INGREDIENTS

- 4 salmon fillets (about 6 oz each)
- 2 tablespoons olive oil
- 2 tablespoons fresh dill, chopped
- 1 lemon, thinly sliced
- 2 garlic cloves, minced
- Salt and pepper to taste
- 1 teaspoon lemon zest
- 1 tablespoon butter, melted (optional)

Fresh parsley for garnish (optional

PREPARATION

- **Preheat the Oven:** Preheat your oven to 375°F (190°C). Line a baking sheet with parchment paper or lightly grease it with olive oil.
- **Prepare the Salmon:** Place the salmon fillets on the prepared baking sheet. Drizzle with olive oil and season each fillet generously with salt and pepper.
- **Add Garlic and Lemon:** Sprinkle the minced garlic over the salmon fillets. Top each fillet with a few lemon slices and sprinkle with fresh dill and lemon zest.
- **Optional Butter Drizzle:** For extra richness, drizzle the melted butter over the salmon fillets before baking.
- **Bake the Salmon:** Bake the salmon in the preheated oven for 12-15 minutes, or until the salmon is opaque and flakes easily with a fork. Cooking times may vary depending on the thickness of the fillets.
- **Garnish and Serve:** Remove the salmon from the oven and garnish with fresh parsley, if desired. Serve with additional lemon wedges for squeezing over the salmon.

8

Vegetarian Stuffed Acorn Squash

INGREDIENTS

- 2 acorn squashes, halved and seeds removed
- 1 cup wild rice, cooked
- ¼ cup dried cranberries
- ¼ cup chopped walnuts or pecans
- 1 tablespoon olive oil
- 1 small onion, chopped
- 1 garlic clove, minced
- 1 teaspoon ground cinnamon
- Salt and pepper to taste

1 tablespoon fresh parsley, chopped (optional)

PREPARATION

- **Preheat the Oven:** Preheat your oven to 400°F (200°C).
- **Roast the Acorn Squash:** Brush the cut sides of the acorn squash halves with olive oil, and season with salt and pepper. Place them cut-side down on a baking sheet and roast for 35-40 minutes, or until the flesh is tender when pierced with a fork.
- **Prepare the Filling:** While the squash is roasting, heat 1 tablespoon of olive oil in a skillet over medium heat. Add the chopped onion and garlic, and sauté until softened, about 3-4 minutes. Stir in the cooked wild rice, dried cranberries, chopped walnuts or pecans, cinnamon, salt, and pepper. Cook for another 2-3 minutes to combine the flavors.
- **Stuff the Squash:** Once the acorn squash is roasted and tender, remove it from the oven and carefully flip the halves over. Spoon the wild rice mixture into each squash half, filling them generously.
- **Optional Additional Bake:** Return the stuffed squash halves to the oven for another 10 minutes to warm everything through.
- **Garnish and Serve:** Remove from the oven, sprinkle with fresh parsley if desired, and serve.

9

Lamb Chops with Rosemary

INGREDIENTS

- 8 lamb chops (about 1 inch thick)
- 2 tablespoons olive oil
- 2 garlic cloves, minced
- 2 tablespoons fresh rosemary, chopped
- 1 teaspoon lemon zest
- Salt and pepper to taste
- 1 tablespoon butter (optional)
- ¼ cup red wine (optional)
- Fresh rosemary sprigs for garnish (optional)

PREPARATION

- **Season the Lamb Chops:** Pat the lamb chops dry with paper towels. Rub both sides of the lamb chops with olive oil, minced garlic, chopped rosemary, lemon zest, salt, and pepper. Let the lamb chops marinate for at least 15-20 minutes, or longer for more flavor.
- **Heat the Pan:** Heat a large skillet or cast-iron pan over medium-high heat.
- **Sear the Lamb Chops:** Once the pan is hot, add the lamb chops. Sear for 3-4 minutes on each side for medium-rare, or cook longer if you prefer them more well-done. The lamb chops should develop a nice golden-brown crust.
- **Optional Butter Baste:** If desired, add 1 tablespoon of butter to the pan during the last minute of cooking and spoon the melted butter over the lamb chops for extra richness.
- **Optional Red Wine Reduction:** If using, remove the lamb chops from the pan and set them aside to rest. Pour the red wine into the pan and deglaze, scraping up the browned bits from the bottom. Simmer for 2-3 minutes until reduced by half. Drizzle the sauce over the lamb chops when serving.
- **Rest and Serve:** Let the lamb chops rest for 5 minutes before serving to allow the juices to redistribute. Garnish with fresh rosemary sprigs if desired.

10

Vegetable Pot Pie

INGREDIENTS

- 1 pie crust (store-bought or homemade)
- 2 tablespoons olive oil
- 1 onion, finely chopped
- 2 garlic cloves, minced
- 1 cup carrots, chopped
- 1 cup green beans, chopped
- 1 cup frozen peas
- 2 tablespoons all-purpose flour
- 1 ½ cups vegetable broth
- ½ cup heavy cream
- Salt and pepper to taste
- 1 teaspoon fresh thyme (optional)
- 1 teaspoon fresh parsley, chopped (optional)
- 1 egg, beaten (for egg wash)

PREPARATION

- **Preheat the Oven:** Preheat your oven to 400°F (200°C).
- **Sauté the Vegetables:** In a large skillet, heat the olive oil over medium heat. Add the onion and garlic, and cook until softened, about 3-4 minutes. Add the chopped carrots and green beans, and cook for another 5-7 minutes until the vegetables start to soften.
- **Make the Creamy Sauce:** Sprinkle the flour over the vegetables and stir to combine, cooking for about 1 minute. Gradually pour in the vegetable broth while stirring to avoid lumps. Bring the mixture to a simmer and cook until thickened, about 3-5 minutes. Stir in the heavy cream, frozen peas, salt, pepper, thyme, and parsley. Cook for another 2 minutes, then remove from heat.
- **Assemble the Pot Pie:** Roll out the pie crust and line the bottom of a pie dish with half of the crust (if using a double crust, reserve the other half for the top). Pour the creamy vegetable mixture into the pie crust.
- **Top with Pie Crust:** If using a top crust, roll it out and place it over the filling. Trim the edges and crimp the crusts together to seal. Cut small slits in the top to allow steam to escape.
- **Egg Wash:** Brush the top of the crust with the beaten egg for a golden finish.
- **Bake:** Bake the pot pie in the preheated oven for 25-30 minutes, or until the crust is golden brown and the filling is bubbling.
- **Cool and Serve:** Allow the pot pie to cool for a few minutes before serving.

Side Dishes

SIDE DISHES

1. <u>Mashed Potatoes</u> — Classic mashed potatoes with butter and cream.
2. <u>Sweet Potato Casserole</u> — Mashed sweet potatoes topped with marshmallows and pecans.
3. <u>Green Bean Casserole</u> — Green beans in a creamy mushroom sauce, topped with fried onions.
4. <u>Roasted Brussels Sprouts</u> — Brussels sprouts roasted with olive oil and garlic.
5. <u>Cranberry Sauce</u> — Fresh cranberries cooked with sugar and orange juice.
6. <u>Cornbread Stuffing</u> — Traditional cornbread stuffing with celery and onions.
7. <u>Glazed Carrots</u> — Carrots glazed with honey and butter.
8. <u>Mac and Cheese</u> — Creamy mac and cheese baked to golden perfection.
9. <u>Garlic Butter Dinner Rolls</u> — Soft, homemade rolls brushed with garlic butter.
10. <u>Caesar Salad</u> — Crisp romaine lettuce with Caesar dressing, croutons, and Parmesan.

Mashed Potatoes

INGREDIENTS

- 2 lbs russet or Yukon gold potatoes, peeled and cut into chunks
- ½ cup unsalted butter
- ½ cup heavy cream (or milk for a lighter version)
- Salt and pepper to taste
- Fresh parsley or chives for garnish (optional)

PREPARATION

- **Boil the Potatoes:** Place the peeled and chopped potatoes in a large pot and cover with cold water. Add a pinch of salt to the water. Bring to a boil over medium-high heat and cook for 15-20 minutes, or until the potatoes are fork-tender.
- **Drain the Potatoes:** Once the potatoes are cooked, drain them well and return them to the pot or a large mixing bowl.
- **Mash the Potatoes:** Using a potato masher, mash the potatoes until smooth. Alternatively, for a creamier texture, you can use a ricer.
- **Add Butter and Cream:** In a small saucepan, warm the butter and cream together until the butter is melted. Gradually add the butter-cream mixture to the mashed potatoes, stirring until smooth and creamy. Add more cream for a softer consistency if desired.
- **Season:** Season the mashed potatoes with salt and pepper to taste. Stir well to combine.
- **Garnish and Serve:** Transfer the mashed potatoes to a serving dish, and if desired, garnish with fresh parsley or chives for a pop of color.

INGREDIENTS

- 4 large sweet potatoes, peeled and cut into chunks
- ½ cup unsalted butter, melted
- ½ cup brown sugar
- ½ cup milk or heavy cream
- 1 teaspoon vanilla extract
- 1 teaspoon ground cinnamon
- ¼ teaspoon ground nutmeg
- ¼ teaspoon salt
- 1 cup mini marshmallows

½ cup chopped pecans

PREPARATION

- **Preheat the Oven:** Preheat your oven to 350°F (175°C).
- **Boil the Sweet Potatoes:** Place the peeled and chopped sweet potatoes in a large pot and cover with water. Bring to a boil over medium-high heat and cook for 15-20 minutes, or until the sweet potatoes are tender when pierced with a fork.
- **Mash the Sweet Potatoes:** Drain the sweet potatoes and transfer them to a large mixing bowl. Mash until smooth using a potato masher or electric mixer.
- **Add Butter and Seasonings:** Stir in the melted butter, brown sugar, milk, vanilla extract, cinnamon, nutmeg, and salt. Mix until well combined and smooth.
- **Assemble the Casserole:** Transfer the mashed sweet potatoes into a greased baking dish. Spread the mixture evenly in the dish.
- **Top with Marshmallows and Pecans:** Sprinkle the mini marshmallows and chopped pecans evenly over the top of the mashed sweet potatoes.
- **Bake:** Bake the casserole in the preheated oven for 20-25 minutes, or until the marshmallows are golden brown and the pecans are toasted.
- **Serve:** Remove from the oven and let cool for a few minutes before serving.

INGREDIENTS

- 1 lb fresh green beans, trimmed (or 2 cans of green beans, drained)
- 1 can (10.5 oz) cream of mushroom soup
- ½ cup milk
- 1 teaspoon soy sauce
- ½ teaspoon black pepper
- 1 cup fried onions (store-bought or homemade)
- 1 tablespoon unsalted butter (optional)
- 1 clove garlic, minced (optional)
- ¼ cup shredded cheddar cheese (optional)

PREPARATION

- **Preheat the Oven:** Preheat your oven to 350°F (175°C).
- **Blanch the Green Beans (If Using Fresh):** Bring a large pot of salted water to a boil. Add the fresh green beans and cook for 4-5 minutes until tender-crisp. Drain the green beans and transfer them to a bowl of ice water to stop the cooking process. Drain again and set aside.
- **Make the Creamy Sauce:** In a mixing bowl, combine the cream of mushroom soup, milk, soy sauce, and black pepper. Stir until smooth.
- **Optional Garlic and Cheese Addition:** For added flavor, sauté the minced garlic in butter over medium heat for 1-2 minutes until fragrant. Add the garlic to the mushroom sauce mixture. You can also stir in shredded cheddar cheese if desired.
- **Assemble the Casserole:** In a large mixing bowl, combine the green beans with the mushroom sauce mixture. Transfer the mixture to a greased 9x13-inch baking dish.
- **Top with Fried Onions:** Sprinkle ¾ cup of the fried onions over the green bean mixture, reserving the remaining ¼ cup for later.
- **Bake:** Bake the casserole in the preheated oven for 25 minutes.
- **Final Onion Topping:** After 25 minutes, remove the casserole from the oven, sprinkle the remaining fried onions on top, and return to the oven. Bake for an additional 5-10 minutes until the onions are golden and crispy.
- **Serve:** Let the casserole cool for a few minutes before serving.

INGREDIENTS

- 1 lb Brussels sprouts, trimmed and halved
- 2 tablespoons olive oil
- 3 garlic cloves, minced
- Salt and pepper to taste
- 1 tablespoon balsamic vinegar (optional)
- 1 tablespoon grated Parmesan cheese (optional)
- Red pepper flakes for garnish (optional)

PREPARATION

- Preheat the Oven: Preheat your oven to 400°F (200°C).
- Prepare the Brussels Sprouts: Trim the ends off the Brussels sprouts and cut them in half. Place them in a large mixing bowl.
- Season the Brussels Sprouts: Drizzle the Brussels sprouts with olive oil, and add the minced garlic. Season with salt and pepper, and toss everything together until the Brussels sprouts are evenly coated.
- Roast the Brussels Sprouts: Spread the Brussels sprouts out in a single layer on a baking sheet. Roast in the preheated oven for 20-25 minutes, or until they are crispy and golden brown on the outside and tender on the inside. Stir halfway through to ensure even cooking.
- Optional Balsamic Glaze: For extra flavor, drizzle the roasted Brussels sprouts with balsamic vinegar during the last 5 minutes of roasting.
- Optional Parmesan Topping: Remove from the oven and sprinkle with grated Parmesan cheese if desired. Garnish with red pepper flakes for a little heat.
- Serve: Transfer the roasted Brussels sprouts to a serving dish and enjoy.

Cranberry Sauce

INGREDIENTS

- 12 oz fresh or frozen cranberries
- 1 cup granulated sugar
- ½ cup fresh orange juice (about 1 large orange)
- 1 teaspoon orange zest (optional)
- ½ cup water
- 1 cinnamon stick (optional)

PREPARATION

- **Combine the Ingredients:** In a medium saucepan, combine the cranberries, sugar, orange juice, water, and orange zest (if using). If you like a warm, spiced flavor, add the cinnamon stick as well.
- **Cook the Cranberries:** Bring the mixture to a boil over medium-high heat. Once boiling, reduce the heat to a simmer and cook for about 10-15 minutes, stirring occasionally, until the cranberries burst and the sauce thickens.
- **Adjust Consistency:** If you prefer a thinner sauce, you can add a little more water or orange juice to reach your desired consistency.
- **Cool the Sauce:** Remove the saucepan from the heat and discard the cinnamon stick (if used). Let the cranberry sauce cool to room temperature—it will continue to thicken as it cools.
- **Chill and Serve:** Once cooled, transfer the sauce to a serving dish and refrigerate for at least 1 hour before serving. Cranberry sauce can be made ahead and stored in the fridge for up to a week.

INGREDIENTS

- **6 cups cornbread, cubed and toasted (store-bought or homemade)**
- **2 tablespoons unsalted butter**
- **1 cup celery, diced**
- **1 cup onion, diced**
- **1 teaspoon fresh thyme, chopped (or ½ teaspoon dried thyme)**
- **1 teaspoon fresh sage, chopped (or ½ teaspoon dried sage)**
- **2 cups chicken or vegetable broth**
- **1 large egg, beaten**
- **Salt and pepper to taste**
- **Fresh parsley for garnish (optional)**

PREPARATION

- **Preheat the Oven:** Preheat your oven to 350°F (175°C). Lightly grease a 9x13-inch baking dish.
- **Toast the Cornbread:** If you haven't done so already, cube the cornbread and toast it in the oven for 10-15 minutes until golden and slightly crispy. This prevents the cornbread from becoming too mushy in the stuffing.
- **Sauté the Vegetables:** In a large skillet, melt the butter over medium heat. Add the diced celery and onion, and sauté for 5-7 minutes, or until softened and fragrant. Stir in the thyme and sage, and cook for another minute. Season with salt and pepper.
- **Combine the Ingredients:** In a large mixing bowl, combine the toasted cornbread, sautéed vegetables, and fresh herbs. Stir gently to combine.
- **Add Broth and Egg:** Pour the chicken or vegetable broth over the cornbread mixture, and stir to moisten the cornbread. Add the beaten egg, and stir gently to combine.
- **Bake the Stuffing:** Transfer the stuffing mixture to the prepared baking dish and spread it out evenly. Cover with aluminum foil and bake for 20-25 minutes.
- **Optional Crisp Topping:** For a crispy top, remove the foil and bake for an additional 10-15 minutes, or until the stuffing is golden and lightly crisp on top.
- **Serve:** Garnish with fresh parsley if desired, and serve warm.

INGREDIENTS

- **1 lb carrots, peeled and cut into 2-inch pieces (or baby carrots)**
- **2 tablespoons unsalted butter**
- **2 tablespoons honey**
- **1 tablespoon brown sugar (optional, for extra sweetness)**
- **1 tablespoon fresh parsley, chopped (optional)**
- **Salt and pepper to taste**
- **1 tablespoon fresh lemon juice (optional, for added brightness)**

Instructions:

PREPARATION

- **Boil the Carrots:** Bring a large pot of salted water to a boil. Add the carrots and cook for 6-8 minutes, or until they are just tender but still firm. Drain and set aside.

- **Make the Glaze:** In a large skillet, melt the butter over medium heat. Stir in the honey, and if using, add the brown sugar for extra sweetness. Let the mixture simmer for 1-2 minutes, stirring constantly, until smooth and slightly thickened.

- **Glaze the Carrots:** Add the cooked carrots to the skillet and toss them in the honey-butter glaze until they are evenly coated. Cook for another 2-3 minutes, allowing the carrots to caramelize slightly. Season with salt and pepper to taste.

- **Add Lemon Juice (Optional):** For a bright, fresh flavor, drizzle the lemon juice over the glazed carrots just before serving.

- **Garnish and Serve:** Transfer the glazed carrots to a serving dish and garnish with fresh parsley if desired.

INGREDIENTS

- 8 oz elbow macaroni (or your favorite pasta)
- 3 tablespoons unsalted butter
- 3 tablespoons all-purpose flour
- 2 cups whole milk
- 1 cup heavy cream
- 2 cups sharp cheddar cheese, shredded
- 1 cup mozzarella cheese, shredded
- ½ cup Parmesan cheese, grated
- ½ teaspoon garlic powder (optional)
- Salt and pepper to taste
- ½ cup breadcrumbs (optional, for topping)
- 1 tablespoon butter (melted, for breadcrumbs)

PREPARATION

- **Preheat the Oven:** Preheat your oven to 350°F (175°C). Lightly grease a 9x13-inch baking dish.
- **Cook the Pasta:** Bring a large pot of salted water to a boil. Add the macaroni and cook according to the package instructions until al dente. Drain and set aside.
- **Make the Cheese Sauce:** In a large saucepan, melt the butter over medium heat. Whisk in the flour and cook for 1-2 minutes, stirring constantly, to form a roux. Gradually add the milk and cream, whisking constantly to avoid lumps. Cook for 4-5 minutes until the sauce thickens.
- **Add the Cheese:** Reduce the heat to low and stir in the cheddar, mozzarella, and Parmesan cheeses. Add garlic powder, salt, and pepper to taste. Stir until the cheese is melted and the sauce is smooth and creamy.
- **Combine Pasta and Sauce:** Add the cooked pasta to the cheese sauce, stirring until the pasta is well-coated with the creamy sauce.
- **Assemble the Mac and Cheese:** Pour the mac and cheese into the prepared baking dish. If using breadcrumbs, mix them with the melted butter and sprinkle over the top of the mac and cheese for a crispy topping.
- **Bake:** Bake in the preheated oven for 20-25 minutes, or until the top is golden and bubbling.
- **Serve:** Let the mac and cheese cool for a few minutes before serving.

Garlic Butter Dinner Rolls

INGREDIENTS

- 3 ½ cups all-purpose flour
- 2 ¼ teaspoons active dry yeast (1 packet)
- 1 cup warm milk (about 110°F)
- 2 tablespoons sugar
- 1 teaspoon salt
- 1 large egg
- ¼ cup unsalted butter, softened
- 2 tablespoons unsalted butter (for brushing)
- 2 garlic cloves, minced (for garlic butter)
- 1 tablespoon fresh parsley, chopped (optional, for garnish)

PREPARATION

- **Activate the Yeast:** In a small bowl, combine the warm milk, sugar, and yeast. Stir and let it sit for 5-10 minutes until the mixture becomes frothy, indicating that the yeast is activated.
- **Make the Dough:** In a large mixing bowl, combine the flour and salt. Add the activated yeast mixture, egg, and softened butter. Stir to combine, then knead the dough for about 8-10 minutes until it is smooth and elastic. You can knead by hand or use a stand mixer with a dough hook attachment.
- **First Rise:** Transfer the dough to a lightly greased bowl, cover with a clean towel or plastic wrap, and let it rise in a warm place for about 1-1 ½ hours, or until doubled in size.
- **Shape the Rolls:** Once the dough has risen, punch it down to release any air. Divide the dough into 12 equal pieces and shape each piece into a ball. Place the dough balls into a greased 9x13-inch baking dish or on a parchment-lined baking sheet.
- **Second Rise:** Cover the rolls with a clean towel and let them rise again for 30-40 minutes, until they are puffy and almost doubled in size.
- **Preheat the Oven:** Preheat your oven to 375°F (190°C).
- **Bake the Rolls:** Bake the rolls in the preheated oven for 15-18 minutes, or until they are golden brown on top.
- **Make the Garlic Butter:** While the rolls are baking, melt 2 tablespoons of butter in a small saucepan over medium heat. Stir in the minced garlic and cook for 1-2 minutes until fragrant. Remove from heat.
- **Brush with Garlic Butter:** When the rolls come out of the oven, immediately brush them with the garlic butter. Garnish with chopped parsley for added flavor and presentation, if desired.
- **Serve:** Serve the garlic butter dinner rolls warm.

10

Caesar Salad

INGREDIENTS

- Ingredients:
- 1 large head romaine lettuce, chopped
- ½ cup freshly grated Parmesan cheese
- 1 cup croutons (store-bought or homemade)
- Fresh black pepper to taste
- Caesar Dressing Ingredients:
- ½ cup mayonnaise
- 2 tablespoons lemon juice
- 1 teaspoon Dijon mustard
- 2 teaspoons Worcestershire sauce
- 2 garlic cloves, minced
- 4 anchovy fillets, minced (optional, but traditional)
- ¼ cup freshly grated Parmesan cheese
- Salt and pepper to taste
- 2-3 tablespoons olive oil (for thinning the dressing, as needed)

PREPARATION

- **Make the Dressing:** In a small bowl, whisk together the mayonnaise, lemon juice, Dijon mustard, Worcestershire sauce, minced garlic, and anchovies (if using). Stir in the Parmesan cheese and season with salt and pepper. Gradually add olive oil, whisking until the dressing is smooth and has your desired consistency. Set aside.

- **Prep the Lettuce:** Wash and thoroughly dry the romaine lettuce. Chop or tear the lettuce into bite-sized pieces and place in a large salad bowl.

- **Assemble the Salad:** Drizzle the Caesar dressing over the lettuce and toss gently to coat. Add more dressing as needed to lightly cover the leaves.

- **Add the Toppings:** Top the salad with freshly grated Parmesan cheese and croutons. Add a sprinkle of black pepper for extra flavor.

- **Serve:** Serve immediately, with extra Parmesan and black pepper on the side if desired.

Desserts

DESSERTS

1. <u>Pumpkin Pie</u> — Classic pumpkin pie with a spiced pumpkin filling.
2. <u>Apple Pie</u> — A traditional apple pie with a flaky crust.
3. <u>Pecan Pie</u> — Sweet and sticky pecan pie with a hint of vanilla.
4. <u>Cranberry Orange Cookies</u> — Soft cookies with dried cranberries and a hint of orange zest.
5. <u>Chocolate Chip Cookies</u> — Classic chocolate chip cookies with gooey centers.
6. <u>Brownies</u> — Fudgy chocolate brownies with a crackly top.
7. <u>Pumpkin Cheesecake</u> — Creamy cheesecake with a spiced pumpkin flavor.
8. <u>Apple Crisp</u> — Baked apples topped with a buttery oat crumble.
9. <u>Sweet Potato Pie</u> — A rich pie made with sweet potatoes, cinnamon, and nutmeg.
10. <u>Bread Pudding</u> — Classic bread pudding with a sweet vanilla sauce.

Pumpkin Pie

INGREDIENTS

- 1 unbaked 9-inch pie crust (store-bought or homemade)
- 1 can (15 oz) pumpkin puree (not pumpkin pie filling)
- ¾ cup granulated sugar
- 2 large eggs
- 1 cup evaporated milk
- 1 teaspoon ground cinnamon
- ½ teaspoon ground ginger
- ¼ teaspoon ground cloves
- ¼ teaspoon ground nutmeg
- ½ teaspoon salt
- Whipped cream for serving (optional)

PREPARATION

- Preheat the Oven: Preheat your oven to 425°F (220°C). Place the unbaked pie crust into a 9-inch pie dish and crimp the edges if desired.
- Make the Pumpkin Filling: In a large mixing bowl, whisk together the pumpkin puree, sugar, eggs, evaporated milk, cinnamon, ginger, cloves, nutmeg, and salt until smooth and well combined.
- Pour the Filling into the Pie Crust: Pour the pumpkin filling into the prepared pie crust, smoothing the top with a spatula if needed.
- Bake the Pie: Bake the pie in the preheated oven at 425°F (220°C) for 15 minutes. Then, reduce the oven temperature to 350°F (175°C) and bake for an additional 40-50 minutes, or until the center of the pie is set and a toothpick or knife inserted into the center comes out clean.
- Cool the Pie: Remove the pumpkin pie from the oven and let it cool on a wire rack for at least 2 hours. This allows the pie to set properly.
- Serve: Once cooled, slice the pumpkin pie and serve with whipped cream if desired.g

Apple Pie

INGREDIENTS

- Pie Crust:
- 2 pie crusts (store-bought or homemade, for a double-crust pie)
- Apple Filling:
- 6-7 Granny Smith or Honeycrisp apples, peeled, cored, and thinly sliced
- ¾ cup granulated sugar
- 2 tablespoons all-purpose flour
- 1 teaspoon ground cinnamon
- ¼ teaspoon ground nutmeg
- 1 tablespoon lemon juice
- 1 tablespoon butter (cut into small pieces)
- For the Top Crust:
- 1 egg, beaten (for egg wash)
- 1 tablespoon granulated sugar (for sprinkling)

PREPARATION

- Preheat the Oven: Preheat your oven to 425°F (220°C). Roll out one pie crust and fit it into a 9-inch pie dish.
- Prepare the Apple Filling: In a large mixing bowl, toss the sliced apples with sugar, flour, cinnamon, nutmeg, and lemon juice until evenly coated.
- Assemble the Pie: Pour the apple filling into the pie crust in the dish, mounding it slightly in the center. Dot the filling with the small pieces of butter.
- Top with the Second Crust: Roll out the second pie crust and carefully place it over the apples. Trim any excess crust, and crimp the edges together to seal. Cut a few small slits in the top crust to allow steam to escape.
- Egg Wash and Sprinkle Sugar: Brush the top of the pie with the beaten egg to give it a golden shine. Sprinkle with granulated sugar for extra sweetness and crunch.
- Bake the Pie: Place the pie on a baking sheet to catch any drips and bake in the preheated oven for 45-50 minutes, or until the crust is golden brown and the apple filling is bubbling through the slits.
- Cool the Pie: Remove the apple pie from the oven and let it cool on a wire rack for at least 2 hours to allow the filling to set.
- Serve: Slice and serve warm or at room temperature. Serve with vanilla ice cream or whipped cream for extra indulgence!

INGREDIENTS

- 1 unbaked 9-inch pie crust (store-bought or homemade)
- 1 cup light corn syrup
- ¾ cup granulated sugar
- 3 large eggs
- 4 tablespoons unsalted butter, melted
- 1 teaspoon vanilla extract
- 1 ½ cups pecan halves
- ¼ teaspoon salt

PREPARATION

- **Preheat the Oven:** Preheat your oven to 350°F (175°C). Place the unbaked pie crust into a 9-inch pie dish and crimp the edges if desired.
- **Make the Pecan Filling:** In a large mixing bowl, whisk together the corn syrup, granulated sugar, eggs, melted butter, vanilla extract, and salt until smooth and well combined.
- **Add the Pecans:** Stir in the pecan halves, making sure they are well coated with the filling mixture.
- **Assemble the Pie:** Pour the pecan filling into the prepared pie crust, spreading the pecans evenly.
- **Bake the Pie:** Bake the pecan pie in the preheated oven for 50-60 minutes, or until the filling is set and the top is golden brown. The pie should slightly jiggle in the center but will firm up as it cools. If the crust starts to brown too quickly, cover the edges with aluminum foil.
- **Cool the Pie:** Remove the pie from the oven and let it cool on a wire rack for at least 2 hours to allow the filling to set.
- **Serve:** Slice the pecan pie and serve with whipped cream or vanilla ice cream if desired.

Cranberry Orange Cookies

INGREDIENTS

- 1 cup unsalted butter, softened
- 1 cup granulated sugar
- 1 large egg
- 2 cups all-purpose flour
- 1 teaspoon baking powder
- ¼ teaspoon salt
- 1 tablespoon orange zest (from 1 large orange)
- 1 tablespoon fresh orange juice
- 1 cup dried cranberries
- ½ teaspoon vanilla extract

PREPARATION

- **Preheat the Oven:** Preheat your oven to 350°F (175°C). Line a baking sheet with parchment paper or a silicone baking mat.
- **Cream the Butter and Sugar:** In a large mixing bowl, cream together the softened butter and granulated sugar using an electric mixer until light and fluffy, about 2-3 minutes.
- **Add the Wet Ingredients:** Beat in the egg, orange zest, fresh orange juice, and vanilla extract until fully combined.
- **Combine Dry Ingredients:** In a separate bowl, whisk together the flour, baking powder, and salt.
- **Mix the Dough:** Gradually add the dry ingredients to the wet ingredients, mixing until just combined. Stir in the dried cranberries.
- **Shape the Cookies:** Using a tablespoon or cookie scoop, drop rounded balls of dough onto the prepared baking sheet, leaving about 2 inches between each cookie.
- **Bake the Cookies:** Bake in the preheated oven for 10-12 minutes, or until the edges are lightly golden. The centers will still be soft but will firm up as they cool.
- **Cool the Cookies:** Remove the cookies from the oven and let them cool on the baking sheet for 5 minutes before transferring them to a wire rack to cool completely.
- **Serve:** Once cooled, enjoy these soft, citrusy cranberry orange cookies with a glass of milk or your favorite warm beverage!

Chocolate Chip Cookies

INGREDIENTS

- 1 cup unsalted butter, softened
- ¾ cup granulated sugar
- ¾ cup brown sugar, packed
- 2 large eggs
- 1 teaspoon vanilla extract
- 2 ¼ cups all-purpose flour
- 1 teaspoon baking soda
- ½ teaspoon salt
- 2 cups semi-sweet chocolate chips
- 1 cup chopped nuts (optional)

PREPARATION

- **Preheat the Oven:** Preheat your oven to 350°F (175°C). Line a baking sheet with parchment paper or a silicone baking mat.
- **Cream the Butter and Sugars:** In a large mixing bowl, cream together the softened butter, granulated sugar, and brown sugar until light and fluffy, about 2-3 minutes.
- **Add the Wet Ingredients:** Beat in the eggs, one at a time, followed by the vanilla extract, until fully combined.
- **Combine Dry Ingredients:** In a separate bowl, whisk together the flour, baking soda, and salt.
- **Mix the Dough:** Gradually add the dry ingredients to the wet ingredients, mixing until just combined. Stir in the chocolate chips and nuts (if using).
- **Shape the Cookies:** Using a tablespoon or cookie scoop, drop rounded balls of dough onto the prepared baking sheet, leaving about 2 inches between each cookie to allow for spreading.
- **Bake the Cookies:** Bake in the preheated oven for 10-12 minutes, or until the edges are golden brown but the centers are still soft. For gooey centers, underbake slightly.
- **Cool the Cookies:** Remove the cookies from the oven and let them cool on the baking sheet for 5 minutes before transferring them to a wire rack to cool completely.
- **Serve:** Enjoy these warm, gooey chocolate chip cookies with a glass of cold milk!

INGREDIENTS

- 1 cup unsalted butter, melted
- 1 cup granulated sugar
- 1 cup brown sugar, packed
- 4 large eggs
- 2 teaspoons vanilla extract
- 1 cup all-purpose flour
- 1 cup unsweetened cocoa powder
- ½ teaspoon salt
- 1 cup semi-sweet chocolate chips (optional)

PREPARATION

- **Preheat the Oven:** Preheat your oven to 350°F (175°C). Grease or line a 9x13-inch baking pan with parchment paper.
- **Mix the Wet Ingredients:** In a large mixing bowl, whisk together the melted butter, granulated sugar, and brown sugar until smooth. Add the eggs, one at a time, whisking well after each addition. Stir in the vanilla extract.
- **Combine the Dry Ingredients:** In a separate bowl, whisk together the flour, cocoa powder, and salt.
- **Mix the Batter:** Gradually add the dry ingredients to the wet ingredients, stirring until just combined. Be careful not to overmix, as this can result in tougher brownies. Fold in the chocolate chips (if using) for extra fudginess.
- **Bake the Brownies:** Pour the batter into the prepared baking pan and spread it out evenly. Bake in the preheated oven for 25-30 minutes, or until a toothpick inserted into the center comes out with a few moist crumbs. The brownies will continue to set as they cool, so slightly underbaking them helps achieve that fudgy texture.
- **Cool the Brownies:** Remove the brownies from the oven and allow them to cool completely in the pan before cutting. This helps create the signature crackly top.
- **Serve:** Once cooled, slice the brownies into squares and enjoy!

7

Pumpkin Cheesecake

INGREDIENTS

- Crust:
- 1 ½ cups graham cracker crumbs
- ¼ cup granulated sugar
- ½ teaspoon ground cinnamon
- 6 tablespoons unsalted butter, melted
- Filling:
- 24 oz cream cheese, softened (3 packages)
- 1 cup granulated sugar
- 1 cup pumpkin puree (not pumpkin pie filling)
- 3 large eggs
- 1 teaspoon vanilla extract
- 1 teaspoon ground cinnamon
- ½ teaspoon ground ginger
- ¼ teaspoon ground cloves
- ¼ teaspoon ground nutmeg
- ¼ cup sour cream

PREPARATION

- **Preheat the Oven:** Preheat your oven to 350°F (175°C). Lightly grease a 9-inch springform pan.
- **Prepare the Crust:** In a medium bowl, combine the graham cracker crumbs, sugar, cinnamon, and melted butter. Press the mixture evenly into the bottom of the prepared springform pan to form the crust. Bake the crust for 8-10 minutes, then remove from the oven and let it cool while preparing the filling.
- **Make the Filling:** In a large mixing bowl, beat the softened cream cheese with an electric mixer until smooth and creamy, about 2-3 minutes. Add the sugar and mix until combined. Add the pumpkin puree, eggs, vanilla extract, cinnamon, ginger, cloves, nutmeg, and sour cream. Beat on medium speed until the mixture is smooth and well-combined.
- **Assemble the Cheesecake:** Pour the pumpkin cheesecake filling over the pre-baked crust, smoothing the top with a spatula.
- **Bake the Cheesecake:** Bake the cheesecake in the preheated oven for 50-60 minutes, or until the center is slightly jiggly but the edges are set. If the top begins to brown too quickly, tent it with aluminum foil.
- **Cool the Cheesecake:** Once baked, turn off the oven and crack the oven door slightly, allowing the cheesecake to cool slowly for 1 hour. This helps prevent cracking.
- **Chill:** Remove the cheesecake from the oven and refrigerate for at least 4 hours, or overnight, to fully set.
- **Serve:** Once chilled, remove the cheesecake from the springform pan and slice. Top with whipped cream if desired.

8

Apple Crisp

INGREDIENTS

- Apple Filling:
- 6 medium apples (Granny Smith, Honeycrisp, or a mix), peeled, cored, and sliced
- 2 tablespoons lemon juice
- ½ cup granulated sugar
- 1 teaspoon ground cinnamon
- ¼ teaspoon ground nutmeg
- 1 teaspoon vanilla extract
- Oat Crumble Topping:
- 1 cup old-fashioned rolled oats
- ¾ cup all-purpose flour
- ½ cup brown sugar, packed
- 1 teaspoon ground cinnamon
- ¼ teaspoon salt
- ½ cup unsalted butter, melted

PREPARATION

- **Preheat the Oven:** Preheat your oven to 350°F (175°C). Lightly grease an 8x8-inch or 9x9-inch baking dish.
- **Prepare the Apple Filling:** In a large bowl, toss the sliced apples with lemon juice, granulated sugar, cinnamon, nutmeg, and vanilla extract. Make sure the apples are evenly coated. Pour the apple mixture into the prepared baking dish.
- **Make the Oat Crumble Topping:** In a separate mixing bowl, combine the oats, flour, brown sugar, cinnamon, and salt. Pour the melted butter over the mixture and stir until the topping forms a crumbly texture.
- **Assemble the Apple Crisp:** Sprinkle the oat crumble topping evenly over the apples.
- **Bake:** Bake the apple crisp in the preheated oven for 40-45 minutes, or until the apples are tender and the topping is golden brown and crispy.
- **Cool and Serve:** Remove from the oven and let the apple crisp cool for 10 minutes before serving. Serve warm with a scoop of vanilla ice cream or a dollop of whipped cream.

9

Sweet Potato Pie

INGREDIENTS

- 1 unbaked 9-inch pie crust (store-bought or homemade)
- 2 cups mashed sweet potatoes (about 2-3 medium sweet potatoes)
- ½ cup unsalted butter, softened
- ¾ cup granulated sugar
- ½ cup brown sugar, packed
- 2 large eggs
- ½ cup evaporated milk
- 1 teaspoon vanilla extract
- 1 teaspoon ground cinnamon
- ¼ teaspoon ground nutmeg
- ¼ teaspoon ground ginger (optional)
- ¼ teaspoon salt

PREPARATION

- **Preheat the Oven:** Preheat your oven to 350°F (175°C). Place the unbaked pie crust into a 9-inch pie dish and crimp the edges if desired.
- **Prepare the Sweet Potatoes:** Peel, boil, and mash the sweet potatoes until smooth. Let them cool slightly before using.
- **Make the Sweet Potato Filling:** In a large mixing bowl, beat together the mashed sweet potatoes and softened butter until smooth. Add the granulated sugar, brown sugar, and eggs, and mix until well combined. Stir in the evaporated milk, vanilla extract, cinnamon, nutmeg, ginger (if using), and salt. Mix until the filling is smooth and creamy.
- **Assemble the Pie:** Pour the sweet potato filling into the prepared pie crust, smoothing the top with a spatula.
- **Bake the Pie:** Bake the pie in the preheated oven for 55-60 minutes, or until the filling is set and a toothpick inserted into the center comes out clean. If the crust begins to brown too quickly, cover the edges with aluminum foil.
- **Cool the Pie:** Remove the pie from the oven and let it cool on a wire rack. The pie will firm up as it cools.
- **Serve:** Serve the sweet potato pie at room temperature or chilled, with a dollop of whipped cream if desired.

10

Bread Pudding

INGREDIENTS

- Bread Pudding Ingredients:
- 6 cups day-old bread (French bread, brioche, or challah), cubed
- 2 cups whole milk
- 1 cup heavy cream
- 4 large eggs
- ¾ cup granulated sugar
- 1 teaspoon vanilla extract
- 1 teaspoon ground cinnamon
- ¼ teaspoon ground nutmeg
- ¼ cup raisins (optional)
- 2 tablespoons unsalted butter (for greasing the dish)
- Vanilla Sauce Ingredients:
- 1 cup whole milk
- ½ cup heavy cream
- ⅓ cup granulated sugar
- 2 large egg yolks
- 1 teaspoon vanilla extract
- 2 tablespoons unsalted butter

PREPARATION

- **Preheat the Oven:** Preheat your oven to 350°F (175°C). Grease a 9x13-inch baking dish with butter.
- **Prepare the Bread Pudding:** Place the cubed bread in the greased baking dish. If using raisins, sprinkle them evenly over the bread cubes.
- **Make the Custard:** In a large mixing bowl, whisk together the milk, heavy cream, eggs, sugar, vanilla extract, cinnamon, and nutmeg until smooth.
- **Assemble the Bread Pudding:** Pour the custard mixture evenly over the bread cubes, pressing the bread down gently to ensure it absorbs the liquid. Let the mixture sit for 10-15 minutes to allow the bread to soak up the custard.
- **Bake:** Bake the bread pudding in the preheated oven for 40-45 minutes, or until the top is golden brown and the custard is set in the center.
- **Make the Vanilla Sauce:** While the bread pudding is baking, prepare the vanilla sauce. In a small saucepan, heat the milk, heavy cream, and sugar over medium heat until it just begins to simmer.
- In a separate bowl, whisk the egg yolks. Slowly pour a small amount of the hot milk mixture into the egg yolks, whisking constantly, to temper the eggs. Then, pour the tempered egg mixture back into the saucepan with the rest of the milk mixture.
- Cook the sauce over medium-low heat, stirring constantly, until it thickens and coats the back of a spoon (about 5-7 minutes). Remove from heat and stir in the vanilla extract and butter until smooth.
- **Serve:** Serve the warm bread pudding drizzled with the sweet vanilla sauce. Enjoy it warm, straight out of the oven, or chilled!

Drinks

DRINKS

1. <u>Hot Apple Cider</u> — Warm spiced apple cider with cinnamon sticks and cloves.
2. <u>Cranberry Spritzer</u> — Cranberry juice mixed with sparkling water and a splash of lime.
3. <u>Pumpkin Spice Latte</u> — A homemade latte with pumpkin puree and warm spices.
4. <u>Spiced Eggnog</u> — Classic eggnog spiced with nutmeg and cinnamon.
5. <u>Mulled Wine</u> — Red wine simmered with spices like cloves, cinnamon, and oranges.
6. <u>Sparkling Cranberry Punch</u> — Cranberry juice, ginger ale, and sparkling water.
7. <u>Hot Chocolate</u> — Rich and creamy hot chocolate topped with whipped cream.
8. <u>Spiced Pear Punch</u> — Pear juice, apple cider, and a touch of cinnamon.
9. <u>Chai Tea Latte</u> — Black tea with milk and chai spices.
10. <u>Pumpkin Smoothie</u> — Pumpkin puree blended with milk, honey, and pumpkin pie spice.

Hot Apple Cider

INGREDIENTS

- **8 cups apple cider (unfiltered is best)**
- **2 cinnamon sticks**
- **4 whole cloves**
- **1 orange, thinly sliced**
- **1 tablespoon whole allspice (optional)**
- **1 tablespoon brown sugar (optional, for added sweetness)**
- **1 teaspoon vanilla extract (optional)**
- **1 star anise (optional, for extra flavor)**
- **Fresh apple slices or cinnamon sticks for garnish (optional)**

PREPARATION

- **Simmer the Cider:** In a large pot, combine the apple cider, cinnamon sticks, whole cloves, sliced orange, and any additional spices like allspice, star anise, or vanilla extract (if using). Stir in the brown sugar if you prefer a sweeter cider.
- **Heat the Cider:** Bring the mixture to a simmer over medium heat, then reduce the heat to low. Let the cider simmer gently for 15-20 minutes, allowing the spices to infuse their flavors into the cider. Stir occasionally.
- **Strain the Cider:** After simmering, strain the hot cider to remove the spices and orange slices. Discard the solids.
- **Serve:** Ladle the hot apple cider into mugs. Garnish with fresh apple slices or an additional cinnamon stick for a festive touch if desired.
- **Optional Serving Tip:** If you'd like to make this an adult beverage, add a splash of bourbon or spiced rum to each mug before serving.

Cranberry Spritzer

INGREDIENTS

- 2 cups cranberry juice (unsweetened or sweetened, depending on your preference)
- 2 cups sparkling water or club soda
- 1 tablespoon fresh lime juice (about 1 lime)
- Ice cubes
- Fresh cranberries and lime slices for garnish (optional)
- 1 tablespoon honey or simple syrup (optional, for added sweetness)

PREPARATION

- Mix the Cranberry and Lime Juice: In a large pitcher, combine the cranberry juice and fresh lime juice. Stir well.
- Add the Sparkling Water: Just before serving, pour the sparkling water or club soda into the pitcher and gently stir to combine.
- Sweeten (Optional): If you prefer a sweeter drink, stir in honey or simple syrup to taste.
- Serve: Fill glasses with ice cubes and pour the cranberry spritzer over the ice. Garnish with fresh cranberries and lime slices for a festive touch.
- Optional Variation: For an adult version, add a splash of vodka or sparkling wine to each glass before serving.

Pumpkin Spice Latte

INGREDIENTS

- 2 cups milk (whole, almond, oat, or any milk of choice)
- 2 tablespoons pumpkin puree
- 1-2 tablespoons sugar (or sweetener of choice)
- 1 teaspoon vanilla extract
- ½ teaspoon pumpkin pie spice (or a mix of cinnamon, nutmeg, ginger, and cloves)
- ¼ cup strong brewed coffee or 1 shot of espresso
- Whipped cream for topping (optional)
- Extra pumpkin pie spice or cinnamon for garnish (optional)

PREPARATION

- **Make the Pumpkin Milk Mixture:** In a small saucepan over medium heat, combine the milk, pumpkin puree, sugar, vanilla extract, and pumpkin pie spice. Stir continuously until the mixture is hot but not boiling. Whisk to ensure the pumpkin puree blends smoothly into the milk.
- **Brew the Coffee:** While the milk is heating, brew a strong cup of coffee or pull a shot of espresso.
- **Combine the Coffee and Pumpkin Mixture:** Pour the brewed coffee or espresso into a mug, then slowly add the hot pumpkin milk mixture. Stir to combine.
- **Top with Whipped Cream (Optional):** If desired, top the pumpkin spice latte with whipped cream and sprinkle with a little extra pumpkin pie spice or cinnamon for a festive touch.
- **Serve:** Enjoy your homemade pumpkin spice latte warm and cozy, perfect for fall mornings or afternoons!

4 *Spiced Eggnog*

INGREDIENTS

- **4 large egg yolks**
- **½ cup granulated sugar**
- **2 cups whole milk**
- **1 cup heavy cream**
- **½ teaspoon ground cinnamon**
- **½ teaspoon ground nutmeg (plus more for garnish)**
- **1 teaspoon vanilla extract**
- **¼ cup bourbon, rum, or brandy (optional, for an adult version)**

PREPARATION

- **Whisk the Egg Yolks and Sugar:** In a medium mixing bowl, whisk together the egg yolks and sugar until the mixture becomes light and creamy.
- **Heat the Milk and Cream:** In a medium saucepan, combine the milk, heavy cream, cinnamon, and nutmeg. Heat the mixture over medium heat until it's hot but not boiling, stirring occasionally.
- **Temper the Egg Yolks:** Slowly pour about ½ cup of the hot milk mixture into the egg yolk mixture, whisking constantly to prevent the eggs from scrambling. Gradually whisk the tempered egg mixture back into the saucepan with the remaining hot milk.
- **Cook the Eggnog:** Continue to cook the eggnog over medium heat, stirring frequently, until it thickens slightly and coats the back of a spoon (about 5 minutes). Do not let the mixture boil.
- **Add Vanilla and Chill:** Remove the eggnog from the heat and stir in the vanilla extract (and alcohol, if using). Let the eggnog cool slightly before transferring it to the refrigerator. Chill for at least 2 hours to allow the flavors to meld.
- **Serve:** Serve the spiced eggnog in glasses, garnished with a sprinkle of ground nutmeg. Add whipped cream if desired for an extra indulgent touch.

Mulled Wine

INGREDIENTS

- 1 bottle (750 ml) red wine (Merlot, Cabernet Sauvignon, or Zinfandel work well)
- 1 orange, sliced into rounds (plus more for garnish)
- ¼ cup honey or sugar (adjust to taste)
- 2 cinnamon sticks
- 4 whole cloves
- 2 star anise (optional)
- 1 teaspoon whole allspice (optional)
- ¼ cup brandy (optional, for extra warmth)
- Fresh cranberries or cinnamon sticks for garnish (optional)

PREPARATION

- **Combine the Ingredients:** In a large saucepan or pot, combine the red wine, orange slices, honey (or sugar), cinnamon sticks, cloves, star anise, and allspice if using.

- **Simmer the Wine:** Heat the mixture over medium heat until it just begins to simmer, but do not let it boil. Once simmering, reduce the heat to low and let the wine gently simmer for 15-20 minutes, stirring occasionally.

- **Optional Brandy Addition:** For a stronger drink, stir in the brandy just before serving.

- **Strain the Wine:** Remove the saucepan from the heat and strain the mulled wine to remove the spices and orange slices.

- **Serve:** Ladle the mulled wine into mugs or heatproof glasses. Garnish with fresh orange slices, cranberries, or a cinnamon stick for a festive touch.

- **Enjoy Warm:** Serve warm and enjoy this cozy, spiced beverage, perfect for winter gatherings and holiday celebrations!

Sparkling Cranberry Punch

INGREDIENTS

- 3 cups cranberry juice (unsweetened or sweetened, depending on preference)
- 2 cups ginger ale
- 1 cup sparkling water or club soda
- 1 tablespoon fresh lime juice (optional, for a citrusy twist)
- Ice cubes
- Fresh cranberries and lime or orange slices for garnish (optional)
- Mint leaves for garnish (optional)

PREPARATION

- **Mix the Cranberry Juice and Lime:** In a large punch bowl or pitcher, combine the cranberry juice and fresh lime juice (if using).

- **Add Ginger Ale and Sparkling Water:** Just before serving, stir in the ginger ale and sparkling water. Stir gently to combine, ensuring the punch stays fizzy.

- **Add Ice and Garnish:** Fill glasses or the punch bowl with ice cubes. Garnish with fresh cranberries, lime slices, or orange slices for a festive look. Add mint leaves for a refreshing touch.

- **Serve:** Pour the punch into glasses and serve immediately while it's still bubbly.

- **Optional Variation:** For an adult version, add a splash of vodka or champagne to the punch for a festive cocktail.

INGREDIENTS

- **2 cups whole milk**
- **½ cup heavy cream**
- **¼ cup unsweetened cocoa powder**
- **¼ cup granulated sugar (adjust to taste)**
- **½ teaspoon vanilla extract**
- **½ cup semi-sweet or dark chocolate chips (or chopped chocolate)**
- **Whipped cream for topping**
- **Chocolate shavings or marshmallows for garnish (optional)**

PREPARATION

- **Heat the Milk and Cream:** In a medium saucepan, combine the milk and heavy cream. Heat over medium heat until the mixture is hot but not boiling.
- **Add the Cocoa Powder and Sugar:** Whisk in the cocoa powder and sugar, stirring until fully dissolved and smooth.
- **Melt the Chocolate:** Add the chocolate chips (or chopped chocolate) to the saucepan and whisk until the chocolate melts completely into the mixture, creating a rich and creamy texture.
- **Add Vanilla:** Stir in the vanilla extract and continue to heat the hot chocolate, but avoid boiling.
- **Serve:** Pour the hot chocolate into mugs. Top with a generous dollop of whipped cream.
- **Optional Garnishes:** Garnish with chocolate shavings, marshmallows, or even a drizzle of chocolate syrup for an extra indulgent treat.

8

Spiced Pear Punch

INGREDIENTS

- **4 cups pear juice (store-bought or fresh-pressed)**
- **2 cups apple cider**
- **1 tablespoon fresh lemon juice**
- **1 teaspoon ground cinnamon (or 2 cinnamon sticks)**
- **1 teaspoon ground nutmeg (optional)**
- **1-2 tablespoons honey or sugar (optional, for added sweetness)**
- **Ice cubes**
- **Pear slices and cinnamon sticks for garnish**

PREPARATION

- **Mix the Juice and Cider:** In a large pitcher or punch bowl, combine the pear juice, apple cider, and fresh lemon juice. Stir well.

- **Add Spices:** Stir in the ground cinnamon and nutmeg (if using). If you're using cinnamon sticks instead of ground cinnamon, add them to the mixture for a more subtle spice infusion.

- **Sweeten (Optional):** If you prefer a sweeter punch, add honey or sugar to taste, and stir until dissolved.

- **Chill or Serve Over Ice:** Chill the punch in the refrigerator for at least 1 hour before serving, or serve immediately over ice cubes for a refreshing, spiced drink.

- **Garnish and Serve:** Pour the spiced pear punch into glasses and garnish with pear slices and cinnamon sticks for a festive touch.

- **Optional Variation:** For an adult version, add a splash of bourbon or rum to each glass for a warming kick.

9

Chai Tea Latte

INGREDIENTS

- 2 black tea bags (or 2 teaspoons loose-leaf black tea)
- 1 ½ cups water
- 1 cup milk (whole, almond, oat, or any milk of choice)
- 1 tablespoon honey or sugar (adjust to taste)
- ½ teaspoon ground cinnamon
- ¼ teaspoon ground ginger
- ¼ teaspoon ground cardamom
- ¼ teaspoon ground cloves
- ¼ teaspoon ground nutmeg
- ½ teaspoon vanilla extract (optional)
- Cinnamon stick or star anise for garnish (optional)

PREPARATION

- **Brew the Tea:** In a medium saucepan, bring the water to a boil. Once boiling, remove from heat, add the black tea bags (or loose-leaf tea in a tea infuser), and steep for 4-5 minutes.
- **Add the Spices:** While the tea is steeping, add the cinnamon, ginger, cardamom, cloves, and nutmeg to the pot. Stir to combine the spices and let them infuse with the tea.
- **Heat the Milk:** In a separate small saucepan, heat the milk over medium heat until warm but not boiling. If you want a frothy chai latte, whisk the milk vigorously or use a milk frother to create foam.
- **Sweeten and Combine:** Remove the tea bags (or strain the loose-leaf tea) from the saucepan. Stir in the honey (or sugar) and vanilla extract (if using) into the spiced tea mixture.
- **Mix the Tea and Milk:** Pour the warm milk into the spiced tea, stirring gently to combine. If you've frothed the milk, spoon the foam on top.
- **Serve:** Pour the chai tea latte into mugs. Garnish with a cinnamon stick or star anise for extra spice and presentation.

10

Pumpkin Smoothie

INGREDIENTS

- ½ cup pumpkin puree
- 1 cup milk (whole, almond, oat, or any milk of choice)
- 1 banana (for creaminess)
- 1-2 tablespoons honey or maple syrup (adjust to taste)
- ½ teaspoon pumpkin pie spice (or a mix of cinnamon, nutmeg, and ginger)
- ½ teaspoon vanilla extract (optional)
- ½ cup Greek yogurt (optional, for extra creaminess and protein)
- Ice cubes (optional, for a chilled smoothie)

PREPARATION

- **Blend the Ingredients:** In a blender, combine the pumpkin puree, milk, banana, honey (or maple syrup), pumpkin pie spice, and vanilla extract (if using). Add the Greek yogurt for a creamier, more protein-rich smoothie.
- **Add Ice (Optional):** If you prefer a chilled smoothie, add a few ice cubes to the blender.
- **Blend Until Smooth:** Blend on high speed until the mixture is smooth and creamy. Adjust the sweetness by adding more honey or maple syrup if needed.
- **Serve:** Pour the pumpkin smoothie into a glass and enjoy immediately.

Thank you so much for choosing the Holiday Treats cookbook.

Wish you will have wonderful cooking moments!

Andrii Pysarenko

Share your creations!

I would like to see your cookwork. Please feel free to share your creations with me on Instagram @andrpys